Contents

2	World Cup Preview	Scotland	34
8	World Cup Map	Wales	37
9	The Draw & Fixtures	Ieuan Evans Profile	40
10	England	Serge Blanco Profile	42
14	Dean Richards Profile	France	44
16	New Zealand	Ireland	47
20	Grant Fox Profile	Simon Geoghegan Profile	50
22	Australia	Rugby Quiz	52
26	Nick Farr-Jones Profile	Argentina to Zimbabwe	54
28	World Cup Stadiums	Rugby Trivia	60
32	Gary Armstrong Profile	Rugby's 'New Age'	62

All information correct as of the end of the Five Nations Championship 1991

Preview

David Kirk (helped by John Kirwan) scores in the corner to help New Zealand to their 29–9 win over France in the first World Cup Final. Auckland, New Zealand – 20th June 1987

It's been billed as the world's third biggest sporting event after the Olympic Games and soccer's World Cup and a glance at the facts and figures of the second rugby World Cup makes it difficult to disagree. 32 matches at 19 different venues around the five host nations . . . most of them playing to packed houses, but generating a worldwide television audience reckoned to top two billion.

That in itself should offer substantial financial bonuses to the game. Despite the recession, a number of major international companies have come in with sponsorship deals in addition to the £3.5 million TV rights fee. The original projection was a £35 million profit; that's had to be adjusted downward, but a more than healthy £20 million is by no means out of the question. The money will go back into the development of the game, for which the 1991 World Cup will be a worldwide promotion; as such, it's a natural extension of the inaugural tournament four years before.

With the benefit of hindsight, the memory of initial doubts about the viability of the first World Cup seems incredible. Would the fans take notice? Would the standard of play match expectations? Would the organisation hold up? In fact, a cumulative TV audience of 250 million watched the event in 18 countries around the world. The misgivings had evaporated long before the final in Auckland in front of 46,000 spectators, as New Zealand defeated France by 29 points to 9. It wasn't the best match of the competition (that had surely been the thrilling semi-final between France and Australia), but it was the fitting end to a successful four weeks, and left the All Blacks as the team to beat next time round.

The holders of the William Webb Ellis Cup open their defence against England at Twickenham on the first day of the tournament. If the predictions of many

Rugby Union

are right, then that same pairing may well also contest the final 30 days later. But the World Cup isn't simply a month long affair; it's taken four years of planning, starting first with the International Rugby Board's decision to stage the tournament across the British Isles and France. Argentina had made a bid and there were suggestions that France – with its high grade facilities – might have taken sole responsibility, but in the event, the IRB eventually arrived at what is effectively a compromise. Certainly, the geographical spread (from Bayonne to Edinburgh) is wide, though no wider than the Tasman Sea that separated venues in 1987.

Rugby World Cup Ltd. was formed to look after all arrangements . . . from tickets to catering, from media coverage to merchandising. But the decision that really mattered to the fans was about who should take part. The 1987 event had been by invitation only, but the strength of the game in the emerging rugby-playing nations demanded either a bigger World Cup competition or a qualifying system. In the end, the format stayed exactly as before, with the Five Nations, New Zealand, Australia and Fiji included by right, and seeded according to where they finished in 1987.

An enthusiastic Wales fan!

That has caused some controversy! England, as losing quarter-finalists in '87, were seeded eighth – Wales, placed third in '87, are number three seeds. Neither seedings appear to reflect current form.

The remaining eight places were open to the ambitions of 21 other Unions around the world. They were required to play in preliminary rounds, and some had to try harder than others! The only abiding tension in the Americas Zone, for

Wales' Steve Sutton and Richard Moriarty battle it out with New Zealand's Gary Whetton in the semi-final at Brisbane – 14th June 1987

example, was over who would end up in Pool 1 with New Zealand and England. Canada, Argentina and the USA were all guaranteed places in the finals . . . they were simply playing for the most favourable draw – won in the end by Canada in Pool 4.

The European Zone was an entirely different matter; there were even preliminary rounds to the preliminary round! A complicated process eventually left Holland and Spain in a four-cornered contest with Romania and Italy, who were previously exempt because of their participation in the 1987 tournament. In the event, the seedings proved justified – Romania and Italy take part again. Altogether 41 preliminary matches were played; the World Cup – in a sense – is already more than halfway complete!

The qualifiers then slotted into a pre-arranged fixture schedule as preparations were made at the selected stadiums. Many grounds, particularly in France, have built new facilities and made available further land to accommodate the media and all varieties of hospitality projects.

There is one abiding concern that may only be resolved once the tournament gets under way . . . the quality of refereeing. There were many criticisms of standards in World Cup '87; for WC '91, referees will be selected by a panel, but the problem of interpretation will remain. Northern Hemisphere referees have different priorities from those of New Zealand and Australia, whose attitudes tend to be more *laissez-faire*. This, doubtless, will be a major issue.

The vast majority of tickets (pool games £4 – £22, with £30 for the best seat at the Final) have been distributed by the appropriate host Union through clubs, in much the same way as they're released for Five Nations matches. Demand is equally high . . . the England v New Zealand match in Pool 1 was sold out early in the year. Hospitality packages have been available of course, but they will be over-subscribed for the best fixtures. If you haven't got a ticket to see your team by now, then it's likely your only hope is through the black market, in itself a risky business.

There's consolation, at least, in the thought that television coverage will be extensive. A year from the start, 58 countries had signed up for pictures, with the host broadcaster ITV set to supply 25 live matches and the remaining seven recorded to its domestic audience in the UK. RTE will do the same in the Republic of Ireland but Screensport will go three better than that with 28 live matches beamed by satellite around Europe.

The rugby world is so confident that the tournament is here to stay, that bids have already been registered by countries hoping to host the RWC in 1995. Even when the timing of South Africa's re-integration into world sport was merely a matter of speculation, the

Australia's Brian Smith throws the ball out as the Japanese can only look on, Sydney – 3rd June 1987

country's rugby authorities were preparing a submission for 1995, although the early indications were that it was unlikely to succeed until 1999.

But for the moment . . . for rugby fans around the world . . . the talk is of '91. Can Australia repeat their recent win over New Zealand . . . will England's Grand Slam propel them to even greater heights . . . will France reproduce their daring, inventive rugby . . . or will New Zealand hang on to their crown?

Sit back . . . and enjoy!

Rory Underwood avoids a Welsh challenge in the quarter-final at Brisbane – 8th June 1987

TOURNAMENT

SCHEDULE 1991

FIXTURES

Date	Kick-off	Match	Venue	Pool	Score
Thursday October 3rd	2.00 3.00	Opening Ceremony England v New Zealand	Twickenham Twickenham	 1	
Friday October 4th	3.00 8.00	Australia v Argentina France v Romania	Llanelli Béziers	3 4	
Saturday October 5th	1.00 3.00 8.00	Italy v USA Scotland v Japan Fiji v Canada	Otley Murrayfield Bayonne	1 2 4	
Sunday October 6th	1.00 3.00	Wales v Western Samoa Ireland v Zimbabwe	Cardiff Arms Park Lansdowne Road	3 2	
Tuesday October 8th	1.00 3.00 8.00	New Zealand v USA England v Italy France v Fiji	Gloucester Twickenham Grenoble	1 1 4	
Wednesday October 9th	1.00 3.00 3.00 5.00 8.00	Australia v Western Samoa Ireland v Japan Scotland v Zimbabwe Canada v Romania Wales v Argentina	Pontypool Lansdowne Road Murrayfield Toulouse Cardiff Arms Park	3 2 2 4 3	
Friday October 11th	3.00	England v USA	Twickenham	1	
Saturday October 12th	1.30 3.15 7.00	Scotland v Ireland Wales v Australia Fiji v Romania	Murrayfield Cardiff Arms Park Brive	2 3 4	
Sunday October 13th	1.00 3.00 8.00	Argentina v Western Samoa New Zealand v Italy France v Canada	Pontypridd Leicester Agen	3 1 4	
Monday October 14th	3.00	Zimbabwe v Japan	Belfast	2	
Saturday October 19th	1.00 3.00	1st Pool 2 v 2nd Pool 3 1st Pool 4 v 2nd Pool 1	Murrayfield Paris	C B	
Sunday October 20th	1.00 3.00	1st Pool 3 v 2nd Pool 2 1st Pool 1 v 2nd Pool 4	Lansdowne Road Lille	D A	
Saturday October 26th	2.30	Winner B v Winner C	Murrayfield		
Sunday October 27th	2.30	Winner A v Winner D	Lansdowne Road		
Wednesday October 30th	2.30	3rd Place Play-off	Cardiff Arms Park		
Saturday November 2nd	2.30	THE FINAL	Twickenham		

All kick off times are PM and local times

Pool 1	**England, New Zealand, USA & Italy.**
Pool 2	**Scotland, Ireland, Japan & Zimbabwe.**
Pool 3	**Wales, Australia, Argentina & Western Samoa.**
Pool 4	**France, Fiji, Canada & Romania.**

World Cup 9

England

England – Grand Slam winners against France at Twickenham – March '91

England scrum-half Richard Hill was full of confidence after that exceptional 21–19 Grand Slam finale against France at Twickenham. "I believe we are capable of winning the World Cup" he said. It was a persuasive view.

England's season had started with a massive 51–0 thrashing of Argentina, but then the team settled back into a more reserved style. England deserved all four of its championship victories because of the power and control of its pack, the tactical supremacy of the half-backs and the record 60 point accuracy of Simon Hodgkinson at full-back. They captured the public imagination to such an extent that captain Will Carling was on BBC's *Wogan* show 48 hours after the French match, sitting in the very same seat that had been occupied by Paul Gascoigne after the other World Cup . . . and as no less recognisable a personality!

And yet, despite the achievements, there had been criticisms. England's remorseless, pack-orientated approach was boring, said the doubters. England, the argument went, were only half the side they could have been; if only they'd used their talented backs as well, then this would have been a spectacular, rather than merely an efficient Grand Slam win.

To support this widely held theory, it was noted that England *lost* the match against France at Twickenham by three tries to one . . . and that only Wales scored fewer tries in the Championship than England's five. Neither Will Carling, nor his partner Jeremy Guscott crossed the line; coach Roger Uttley remarked in his review of the season that his main concern was the team's seeming inability to convert good possession into tries.

England's conservatism had been born a year before at Murrayfield, where their 1990 Grand Slam bid died after a season of extravagant try-scoring. The frustrations of the Scottish defeat steeled them to a fiercer determination for 1991. Results became all-important, words like "pressure" became common currency in their desperation to win.

Yet there were signs, both during and after the France game, that the "boring" tag was beginning to rankle. Despite the rain, England attempted to run the ball more than in any of the other three games, Rory Underwood's try was a delight and Hill's prophesy after the match was for "a more expansive game" during the World Cup.

Hill's stand-off partner Rob Andrew added "We have always said that the championship was the stepping-stone". His belief is that England must improve before the World Cup and the interim tour of Australia and that Fiji was designed to help them do just that. England took a 30 man squad, having announced beforehand that matches may be lost on the way, particularly since some experimentation would take place with the side.

The beauty of Five Nations 1991 for England was that experimentation hadn't been necessary. The same 15 played uninjured throughout the campaign and the natural benefits accrued; understanding, confidence and good team morale, despite the irritation over the issue of payment for off-the-field activities.

The Grand Slam also effectively kept them together for the World Cup, as defeat against France might well have caused the ageing pack to break up. Now it seems that only injury or severe loss of form in Australia will prevent the formidable Dooley/Ackford second row combination from dominating World Cup line-outs and binding the pack into a unit of mobility and power to match the All Blacks. Dean Richards, at number 8, was widely regarded as England's player

Nigel Heslop avoids Moore's ....

.... tackle to score against Scotland at Twickenham – February '91

of the championship – a remarkable achievement in a year of comeback from injury. These are the world-class names in a pack of proven strength and skill. The key elements of possession, drive, discipline and pressure combined to make an outstanding force that either scored points (flanker Mike Teague got two championship tries) or created such havoc that penalties were constantly forthcoming.

The half-back combination of Hill/Andrew was also a major plus for England. Although Hill directed the game as much with his boot as with his hands, this was still an intelligent partnership, which built on the forward platform. Andrew kicked more than he passed, but his awareness and skill constantly resulted in territorial advantage. These were vital elements as England turned the screw.

Of course, the disappointment was in the centre. In 1990 Will Carling and Jeremy Guscott had scored six championship tries between them – in 1991 neither had crossed the line. Yet the considered end-of-season view emphasised not so much how they'd been wasted, but just what England had in reserve for the World Cup. No-one can doubt their ability. If England's strategy is adjusted away from safety-first, then their contributions will be significant.

Rory Underwood stands out as the senior winger. Nigel Heslop played his part in the win over Scotland with a try but Underwood's 27 tries in 43 matches (he scored against Ireland and France) by the end of the championship, puts him way ahead in experience and right at the top of the danger list.

And so to the man who says training is boring! Simon Hodgkinson's right foot swung so consistently during the first half of the season that it was obvious that penalties meant points. He was less consistent against Ireland and France, but still his 15 points per game average broke international records and became more than just a platform for victory. It became victory itself! He rates alongside New Zealand's Grant Fox as a major points accumulator for the World Cup.

Mike Teague holds on as Jean-Pierre Garuet tackles at Parc Des Princes – February '90

So how realistic is the challenge of the Northern Hemisphere champions? The draw won't reward them if they stun the rugby world by defeating New Zealand to qualify for the quarter-finals as Pool 1 winners. They'd probably have to beat Australia and New Zealand (again) to win the World Cup. If they qualify for the quarter-finals as Pool 1 runners-up, then the draw would probably take them to play France in Paris and then Scotland at Murrayfield before the final.

Beyond the difficulties of the route, there's a substantial question-mark over the quality of the players in reserve. The England "B" team is not a formidable outfit, so the first-choice players will need to keep their form and fitness. But on the credit side, they have a solid, stable management structure headed by Geoff Cooke, with real ability on the pitch . . . and real self-belief!

They've peaked once in 1991 . . . to reach a second summit before the team, inevitably, breaks up would be a fantastic achievement.

Wade Dooley is first to the ball against Argentina at Twickenham – November '90

Dean Richards

If England owed its Grand Slam more to its pack than to its backs, then the pack owes a large part of its success to the revitalised form of number eight Dean Richards. At 6ft 4in and only the *third* tallest member of the scrum, 'Big Deano' answered all the fears about his return from injury, with four consistent displays of power and authority in England's season. It followed the void of 1989/90, when he was completely side-lined with a shoulder injury sustained during the last game of the Lions' tour of Australia in 1989.

Richards was educated at John Cleveland College, Hinckley and played for England Schools at lock before spending a year in France, where he completed his first senior season with Roanne. Then, in 1982, he started his long associated with Leicester, working his way through the Midlands divisional team and England under-23s to a first full cap in 1986 against Ireland, where he scored two debut tries.

Richards once made the headlines more for what he did off the field than for what he did on it (the infamous game of touch rugby with the Calcutta Cup in the streets of Edinburgh!). However, that was not typical of Richards as he is hardly the extrovert type. His qualities are those of quiet determination and courage, both of which have served him well in his frequent struggles against injury.

Fortunately for both England and the Lions, he has always been able to give his best on the big occasion. He's a highly astute tactician, interpreting the game from its very heart and is as capable in attack as in defence (he's averaged only just under a point per match for England). He will be a vital figure for his country as they face up to New Zealand in those first, fierce moments of the tournament.

Dean RICHARDS (ENGLAND)

Born: 11th July 1963
Height: 6ft 3½in
Weight: 17st 3lbs
Occupation: Police officer
Position: No. 8
Club: Leicester
International debut: 1986 v Ireland
Caps: 25
International Points: 24 (6 tries)
Other honours: 3 British Lions caps

New Zealand

World Champions, favourites, the most powerful, most respected team in the world, the All Blacks come to the 1991 World Cup just as they left it in 1987 when Captain Kirk boldly went where no man had gone before . . . to collect the William Webb Ellis Cup.

Craig Innes fends off Ireland's ....

Nothing short of comprehensive defeat by Australia in the 1991 Bledisloe Cup series will prevent the pre-tournament view that New Zealand must emerge again as champions.

And yet, there's been no concealing that Alex "Grizz" Wyllie's side has passed through a period of vulnerability since June '87 in Auckland. In the Southern Hemisphere's winter of 1990, Scotland, fresh from their Grand Slam, had a second Test victory in their grasp at Eden Park, Auckland, leading by nine points before finally going under 21–18.

The look of utter All Black invincibility was slipping. It finally fell away just over a year before WC '91 in Wellington and with it went an unbeaten record stretching back 50 matches to late 1986. The by now historic 3rd Test result was New Zealand 9, Australia 21. The All Blacks had already taken the series but this was still a painful defeat, and with it came the doubts over the captaincy of Gary Whetton and the rejection of the previously dominant Wayne Shelford.

There was also generally disappointing form behind the scrum and a specific problem behind the scenes as Wyllie and his fellow-selector John Hart simply didn't get on! The chairman of the NZRFU Eddie Tonks went public on a row which eventually

....Philip Rainey at Lansdowne Road – November '89

ended with Hart satisfying his ambitions with the New Zealand Colts, while Wyllie took on Lane Penn as assistant. But not before more problems!

In late 1990, New Zealand's tour of France got off to the worst possible start with one defeat in their first provincial

The New Zealand Squad at Parc des Princes, Paris – November '90

match in Toulon, and then another in Bayonne. This unprecedented setback nevertheless left Wyllie with his own sense of perspective, "We lost against Australia, but if we lose two matches in France, but go on to win the Tests and then retain the World Cup, then those defeats will have signified absolutely nothing."

And so it may well prove. In the event, both Test Matches were convincingly won. In Nantes, a disgracefully over-physical game (with the French substantially to blame) was taken by 24 points to 3, with Grant Fox kicking 16 points and proving, once again, his immense value to the side. Innes and Alan Whetton scored the tries. The pack played with impressive authority and control . . . and repeated the performance for the second Test in Paris. 30–12 to the All Blacks, this time six penalties and two conversions to Fox, with Crowley and Jones the try scorers.

The All Blacks had wobbled early on, but emerged with their reputation intact, looking forward to close observation of the 1991 Five Nations Championship for an assessment of comparative strengths.

Just seven of the team for the 2nd Test in Paris had played in the World Cup Final three years or so before, and many of them are likely to consider retirement immediately after this World Cup. So this is a side in a state of transition, to some extent holding on for November 2nd 1991, and still regretting the departure of several big names to Rugby League.

John Gallacher's departure was, of course, the biggest. He left Wellington for Leeds and about £400,000 in the summer of 1990, a move that left Wyllie stunned. "You're joking!" was his response, but Gallacher wasn't and neither were Matthew Ridge, John Schuster or Frano Botica. Wyllie's more considered reaction later was that "their experience and knowledge were sorely missed." He clearly didn't feel the same about number 8 Wayne Shelford, the colossus of the 1987 World Cup, who was dropped after the Scotland match through lack of fitness. The outspoken

Zinzan Brooke scores against the Barbarians at Twickenham – November '8

Craig Innes dives over the line to score his first try against Wales at Cardiff Arms Park – November '

Shelford disputed the coach's view, but he was still omitted for the French tour. Early this year, the 33 year-old Shelford was still setting his sights on re-selection for the World Cup squad, even as captain! He's got one useful statistic up his sleeve, he has never led a New Zealand side to defeat in his 14 matches in charge.

But from the *Improbables* to the *Impossibles to Ignore*. Flanker, Michael Jones will be absolutely vital to the All Black campaign. The true discovery of the 1987 tournament very nearly lost his ability to walk, let alone play, when he severely damaged a knee against Argentina in 1989. But approaching the World Cup, Jones appeared to be back in great form.

Indeed the whole pack had an extremely settled look to it as the 1991 Bledisloe Cup series with Australia approached. Who could possibly argue that the McDowell/Fitzpatrick/Loe front row isn't the best in the world, with the Whettons; Alan, and Gary still prominent? Add Jones and that's a formidable, experienced nucleus for a World Cup winning scrum, with Loe the only absentee from the 1987 final.

The immensely reliable talent of stand-off Grant Fox – an Auckland player, along with half of the team – will bring valuable points and Terry Wright, Craig Innes and John Kirwan are expected to stand out in the back division.

Much will be expected of New Zealand. Immediately. The opening Pool 1 match against England at Twickenham is potentially the final too. Defeat in front of Twickenham's intensely patriotic crowd could store psychological damage for later in the tournament.

For the doubters, nothing less than convincing victory will do. Against England . . . against everybody!

Graeme Bachop at Parc des Princes - November '90

Grant Fox

The statistics speak for themselves. By the end of New Zealand's 1990 tour of France, Grant Fox had scored an amazing international average of almost 16 points per match. Despite Simon Hodgkinson's record 60 points for England in this year's Five Nations championship, Fox remains the world's undisputed number one goal-kicker, and his boot, the New Zealand match winner.

This was no more self-evident than in the 2nd Test against Scotland in Auckland last year. New Zealand scored one try to the Scots' two, but Fox – obliged to aim mostly from the touch-line – succeeded with all six kicks at goal to pull the game round by 21 points to 18.

And then, on that tour to France, Fox was absent from the first two matches against provincial sides. Result? . . . the All Blacks lost them both! With Fox back in the side for the two Test Matches, New Zealand won them both. His contribution was 38 points! Ironically, Fox believes that try scoring is what the game is all about and that the penalty is too valuable at three points, he'd prefer to see it worth two!

But his kicking for position is almost as demoralising as his kicking for goal, it's the source of New Zealand's high pressure forward play. Flankers throughout the world have tried to hunt Fox down, but only one – the Australian Scott-Young – managed to catch him to cause a rare All Black defeat. That was in the Third Test of the 1990 Bledisloe Cup Series, which, by then, the All Blacks had already won!

The world has the former Wales international Barry John to thank for Grant Fox, who watched John as a boy on the 1971 Lions tour of Wales. His ambition was born and he worked his way through the New Zealand Schools XV, Auckland University XV and then to the Auckland club. He became the All Blacks' first choice outside-half during the 1987 World Cup. The rest is methodical, accurate history, well-documented enough to assert that Fox can win the Cup (again!) for New Zealand!

Grant FOX (NEW ZEALAND)

Born: June 16th 1962
Height: 5ft 8in
Weight: 11st 11lbs
Occupation: Company representative
Position: Fly-half
Club: Auckland
International debut: 1985 v Argentina
Caps: 27
International points: 430 (1 try, 76 penalties, 90 conversions, 6 drop goals)
Other honours: He holds New Zealand's record for international points scored

Australia

Australia set fair

The English winter – and Australian summer – of 1990/91 was more than just a good memory for Aussie sports fans – it was something approaching the ultimate glory! While the Kangaroos were pulling back a one-match deficit to take the Rugby League series 2–1 against Great Britain, Alan Border's men were humiliating England's cricketers in the Ashes Series by three Tests to nil. English Rugby Union fans must be breathing a huge collective sigh of relief that England and Australia can't meet until the World Cup semi-finals at the very earliest!

But will Australia get that far, and if they do, will their involvement end there as it did so gloriously in the thrilling 1987 semi-final defeat by France, which has often been described as the greatest ever-rugby international? On recent form the likely answers are "yes" and "probably"!

Australia, seeded fourth, are rated as second or third best side in the tournament, depending on which *bookie* you speak to! The team's belief may go beyond even that! It was the Wallabies, after all, who inflicted the first defeat on an All Blacks side in four years with their 1990 3rd Test win in Wellington by 21 points to nine. That was clearly a match in which everything came right to a scrum which performed with aggressive consistency . . . and to the outside-half pairing of Nick Farr-Jones and Michael

Lynagh, which at last – after their side's two previous Bledisloe Cup defeats – had rediscovered their famous understanding. It allowed Australia to upgrade their World Cup pretensions, which were already substantial after an earlier Test series win against France on home soil.

Yet off the field, the 12 months preceding the World Cup had not been without problems, starting with a bitter coup of the previous selectors. A controversial ballot ousted the incumbents, John Bain and Bob Templeton, who were long-serving and anticipating the World Cup as a swan-song. The team manager Andy Conway was also dismissed. In their place came a new chairman Bob Dwyer from New South Wales and the Queensland coach John Connolly with Barry Want making up the new selection panel.

Then later came an issue which threatened to divide the new panel itself, that of the charismatic try-scorer David Campese. "Campo" – as usual – played the 1990/91 season in Italy with Milan, and argued that he should stay in Europe after the ARFU deadline for returning players in the first week of April. This, despite the fact that a similar move a year earlier had prevented his selection for the 1st Test against France.

Dwyer was largely sympathetic, but Connolly's views on the importance of getting players back in time for representative teams (and thus in tune for Test Matches) was well known.

David Campese

Greg Martin and Jeff Miller jump with Gavin Hastings at Sydney — July '89

Since other lesser lights in the Australian set-up had made it clear that they were happy to comply with the deadline, it potentially raised the divisive issue of one law for the rich and another for the poor, just at the moment that Australia needed a united run-in to the World Cup!

However, it didn't prevent Campese being named in the Wallabies' preliminary 36-man World Cup training squad . . . though the interesting question of where Campese should put his immense talent to best use was still unresolved. This brilliant, but erratic player (remember his dreadful mistake against the British Lions in the 1989 decisive 3rd Test?) was named as one of five wingers, despite the fact that he'd played two out of three Tests against the All Blacks at full-back. The theory is that the number 15 shirt gives him greater freedom. He's impossible to omit, but when he plays is it on a wing . . . or a prayer?!

Michael Lynagh scored 32 points in the three All Black Tests, certainly a respectable haul, though there was some criticism of his tactical kicking in the two defeats. But the outstanding personality of the Australian "Big Three" names is undoubtedly the captain Nick Farr-Jones. Off the field, he's a Sydney solicitor, a popular man who's in demand as much on the golf course as at dinners and functions. On the field, he's already the country's most capped scrum-half and now an astutely intelligent captain. When the experienced combination of Farr-Jones and Lynagh operates on the same wavelength, then Australia truly are world-beaters.

In a team which has recently undergone many changing combinations, one area of potential consistency during the World Cup build-up is in the front row. Tony Daly, Phil Kearns (try-scorer in the victory against the All Blacks) and Ewen McKenzie are likely to prove formidable opponents in Pool 3 and beyond. They play their part in the Wallabies' tougher approach to their game, along with the newly arrived Villiame ("Willie") Ofshengaue. He's from Tonga, but has qualified for Australia and can play either number eight or flanker. In the backs, inside-centre Tim Horan stands out. He played the entire New Zealand series with an injury, but was fiercely competitive nevertheless.

So, to return to the original question, the answer is "yes"! Australia will surely win Pool 3 and – in their quarter final – overcome the runners-up in Pool 2 (Ireland?) to appear in another semi-final. Their opponents? . . . almost certainly New Zealand, unless England have caused a sensation in Pool 1. Hence the answer of "probably".

Unless, of course, you believe that lightning can strike twice!

Nick Farr-Jones clears the ball from a ruck against New Zealand – August '89

Nick Farr-Jones

The early story of Nick Farr-Jones (widely regarded as the best scrum-half in the world), is of what might have been lost to the game. His first winter sport was soccer, but he couldn't even make his school team first XV (at Newington College in New South Wales.) He played just one season of Colts rugby before moving into the senior grade game in Sydney.

But it was here (in the city's second division) that his career took off, helping him gain access to the Australian Universities side with which he toured Britain in 1983. He was back a year later for the greatest kick-start a full international career could ever have. The Wallabies won a magnificent Grand Slam on their 1984 British tour. Farr-Jones made his debut in the 19–3 win over England at Twickenham and stayed in the side for the other three victories.

Other milestones, included the 2–1 Test series win over New Zealand in 1986, but – since being awarded the captaincy which he has kept since 1988 – there have been low-points too, especially the 1989 2–1 series defeat by the British Lions. He's been hit, literally, from all sides. He played part of the second test in that series with a bloody, swollen mouth after taking a punch full in the face. Since then there's been sniping from fellow-players and observers about his captaincy, criticisms which he's found hurtful and misplaced.

Most would agree with him as he's generally well-liked in his hometown of Sydney, where he works as a solicitor, specialising in property. His power of argument makes a persuasive case in the on-going controversy over the game's amateurism laws, which he believes to be out-dated. His voice has been one of the Southern Hemisphere's loudest, in protest at the inconsistencies created by the International Rugby Board.

Nevertheless, Farr-Jones will doubtless agree that the IRB has got the World Cup right, especially if he leads his side towards (and perhaps even beyond) a semi-final with New Zealand!

Nick FARR-JONES (AUSTRALIA)

Born: April 14th 1962.
Height: 6ft
Weight: 13st 8lbs
Occupation: Solicitor
Position: Scrum-half
Club: Sydney University
International debut: 1984 v England
Caps: 44
International points: 32 (8 tries)
Other honours: By the end of 1990 his 20 matches captaining his country was a national record. He is also his country's most capped scrum-half

Rugby Union

The Stadiums

The 1991 World Cup matches are being played at nineteen different grounds – from Belfast to Béziers. Here we profile the five major grounds – each with their own special characteristics and individual atmosphere.

Action in front of the new North Stand

TWICKENHAM, LONDON

In 1907, the Rugby Football Union finally solved the problem it had been struggling with for years . . . the establishment of a permanent home ground for England's international fixtures. Some ten acres of market garden near Twickenham, in those days little more than the size of a village, was bought for the sum of £5,572 12s. 6d. Since then, it's been a story of continuing expansion and development; Twickenham, the venue for the 1991 World Cup Final, now vies only with the Sydney Football stadium for the title of the most impressive Rugby Football ground in the world.

The first match at Twickenham was played at the beginning of the 1909/10 season and was between Harlequins and Richmond . . . the first international was played on January 15th 1910, between England and Wales. England won 11–6, watched by a crowd of approximately 20,000. After a lull during the First World War, the ground grew way beyond its original conception, so that by 1936, a crowd of 73,000 were watching England play the All Blacks. By then the ground had stands on three sides; on the south side was a large terrace which, alone, was capable of taking some 20,000 fans.

Looking towards the South Stand

Apart from some modifications to the South Terrace, the ground stayed much the same throughout the 50's and 60's, but the continuing pressure on space and demand for better facilities eventually resulted in the completion, in 1981, of the South Stand for just over £5 million. This, in itself, offered a glimpse of what was possible at rugby's headquarters . . . a modern, imposing structure with excellent viewing facilities, but which nevertheless stood out in a ground which was essentially old-fashioned.

Once England had won the go-ahead to stage the 1991 World Cup, an ambitious project for the complete rejuvenation of Twickenham was unveiled by the Rugby Union. The Sheffield architects Husband and Co. were commissioned to produce designs for modernising the remaining three sides of the stadium and in November 1988 they produced a spectacular vision for the future, that of an all-seater stadium with 75,000 capacity, to be completed shortly after the turn of the century in three stages.

The first stage, the new North Stand, is already finished at a cost of £16 million. It's a fabulous three tier structure, complete with executive boxes, and has a height of over a hundred feet. It holds 15,000 spectators and was opened in time for the 1990 Varsity match.

The anticipated completion of stages two and three (new East and West Stands to form a horseshoe shape with the North) has already elevated Twickenham to the status of England's premier sports stadium for the 21st century. The Football Association were so impressed by both the viewing and conference facilities in the plans that it's likely they will offer the ground as a venue in any bid for future international soccer tournaments. Even if the 1998 World Cup isn't held in England, it's quite possible that the FA might eventually abandon Wembley for Twickenham to stage internationals and FA Cup Finals.

And beyond that? Hockey, tennis, even American football might eventually find a home at Twickenham. The traditionalists in this most traditional of all sports might well blanch at the thought, but the fact is that the Rugby Union is living in the modern world. The total development cost of some £75 million couldn't be met by rugby alone, not even in these boom years. By all accounts, Twickenham has a great future!

CARDIFF ARMS PARK, CARDIFF

The first match played on the site of Cardiff Arms Park was by Cardiff RFC in 1876, nine years after the ground was first used for cricket. The first international was in 1884 against Ireland, won by Wales with a drop goal and two tries to nil. The ground was developed with stands and larger terracing throughout the 20th century until – in 1967 – the WRFU acquired the freehold. The cricket pitch was then moved to Sofia Gardens and the new National Stadium started to take shape. Completed in 1982, it has already staged international soccer matches and there are plans for the Welsh FA to use it on a regular basis. Its current capacity is 56,000 but crowds of well over 60,000 were recorded before the installation of extra seating.

PARC DES PRINCES, PARIS

The Parc des Princes was built as France's national stadium for soccer, rugby union and rugby league. Its first ever match was the French FA Cup Final of 1972, but the first rugby union fixture to be played there was Béziers v Neath on November 1st 1972. The first international came two months later with France v Scotland on January 13th 1973. Since the stadium was opened, its current capacity of 49,700 has been frequently achieved.

LANSDOWNE ROAD, DUBLIN

Lansdowne Road is the oldest international ground in the world. The first match played there took place in 1876 against England. The highest ever attendance has never been recorded but there were regular crowds of approximately 60,000 before recent safety legislation reduced the capacity to 50,000, with 24,000 seats. It is also one of the busiest grounds in the British Isles, with two club sides using it as a home ground, as well as the Republic of Ireland soccer team.

MURRAYFIELD, EDINBURGH

The first ever match at Murrayfield was played on March 21st 1925, with Scotland (in a Grand Slam year) beating England by 14 points to 11. In 1959, the Murrayfield pitch was the first in Scotland to be installed with electrically-powered undersoil heating. It's been replaced with a gas system during the last close season, but the pitch is to be re-turfed in plenty of time for the start of the World Cup. The biggest ever attendance at Murrayfield was a massive 104,000 (a world record for rugby) which crammed in for the match against Wales on March 1st 1975. The current capacity is 54,000, with 31,000 seats.

World Cup **31**

Gary Armstrong

Gary Armstrong will be one of the outstanding scrum-halves of the World Cup. *That* much seems sure as the team's uncertain 1991 Championship form provides the context for Scotland's challenge. The Jed-Forest and Scotland scrum-half hasn't looked back since his debut in 1988 and admirers have seen promise quickly transformed into achievement.

The highlight of his career so far has obviously been the 1990 Grand Slam, but his accomplishments in the two narrowly-lost Test Matches in New Zealand later that year enhanced his developing reputation as a scrum-half with all the relevant talents. A considerable asset to his strong running is his sturdy physique (he was an agricultural labourer before becoming a lorry driver), but his kicking is also accurate and he reads the game especially well.

He's worked closely with the former Jed-Forest and Scotland scrum-half Roy Laidlaw in developing his game and he's gone to the top of Scottish rugby in tandem with his half-back partner Craig Chalmers, who has just two caps less than him. It was no coincidence that their rise synchronised with an upturn in the Scottish game. The names 'Armstrong and Chalmers' fused as one of those stable, sporting partnerships. It's now the fulcrum of the Scottish side.

Since then, there have been the comparative, collective disappointments of 1991, but Armstrong's form did not perceptibly diminish. His contribution to Scotland's win over Wales included a try and his dominance over opposite number Robert Jones led to Jones being dropped. (Jones had kept Armstrong out of the Lions' Test Matches in Australia in 1989.) All this, despite the fact that he had to recover from a knee injury in late 1990 to make the side.

In contrast to his evident commitment on the field, his off-field personality is calm and down-to-earth. For instance, he doesn't appear to have the material ambitions that might tempt him away to Rugby League. The overall impression of Gary Armstrong, is of a man who loves the game and its challenges, especially his first World Cup! And – for the record – he thinks Scotland can win it!

Gary Armstrong (Scotland)

Born: September 30th 1966
Height: 5ft 10in
Weight: 12st 11lbs
Occupation: Lorry driver
Position: Scrum-half
Club: Jed-Forest
International debut: 1988 v Australia
Caps: 18
International points: 12 points (3 tries)

Scotland

Scotland wing Tony Stanger takes on the Welsh defence at Murrayfield - February '90

Once again the cry "Scotland for the World Cup!" is being heard up and down the land. A cry that's appeared in a different sporting context from Genoa to Cordoba, and from Frankfurt to Seville. Had it been shouted from the terraces of Murrayfield after Scotland's historic 1990 Grand Slam, then – for the first time – it might not have been entirely unrealistic! That 13–7 win over England was the result of the determined, disciplined rugby that was inevitable from the moment David Sole led his men onto the pitch in that slow, menacing stride and it set Scotland up for their successful summer tour of New Zealand.

There they won five and drew one of their provincial matches, and so nearly overcame the All Blacks in the second of their two Test Matches, scoring two tries to the All Blacks' one and leading at half-time before eventually going down 18–21. Beyond that, the tour was regarded as excellent experience for the many younger players that made up the party of 30, all of whom made their contributions in those successful

34 *Rugby Union*

provincial matches. It was regarded at the time as a tour that consolidated the achievements of the past, and laid down the foundations for success in the future.

A massive 49–3 annihilation of Argentina followed in the autumn of 1990, but then came the Five Nations Championship of 1991 . . . and – if not disaster – then severe disappointment. Scotland, it seemed, had peaked too early!

The fixture list threw them into the

Gavin Hastings jumps against Jeremy Guscott at Twickenham – February '91

championship at the deep end with their first match against France in Paris, where they hadn't won for 22 years . . . and where the run continued with a 15–9 defeat in a largely bad-tempered and mediocre match. An emphatic 32–12 win over Wales at Murrayfield followed a fortnight later but signified little! Then came the grudge match against

David Sole – bloodied, but unbowed

England at Twickenham, in which the Calcutta Cup was conceded by 21 points to 12. Scotland's season was effectively over, even that late but narrow win over Ireland left more questions than answers. Scotland still remain favourites to win Pool 2, but only just!

They have had the summer to regroup and to think beyond the World Cup from the front-row was certainly an inspiration during the Grand Slam, and although the pack was seen to falter in '91, it contains a potentially formidable back-row, in Turnbull, White and John Jeffrey (the "White Shark"). The young half-back pairing of Gary Armstrong and Craig Chalmers should still be intact for the World Cup, and the Hastings

The Scotland Squad against Wales at Murrayfield – February '91

achievements that are merely expected of them, to their ultimate ambitions. Winning Pool 2 would give them another match at Murrayfield – probably against Wales – from which they would naturally be expected to proceed to a semi-final (again on home soil), probably against either England or France. So the draw has been kind to the Scots, giving them the real possibility of playing all their matches at Murrayfield, and avoiding both New Zealand and Australia, right through to the final itself!

On the basis that good players don't suddenly become bad, the Scottish squad is still likely to contain the big names that featured over the differing seasons of 1990 and 1991. David Sole's leadership brothers, Scott and Gavin, will also feature. Gavin, especially, is a highly valuable asset at full-back, a try-scorer who can also share the kicking duties with Chalmers if required.

The key to Scottish success, though, may lie behind the scenes in coach Ian McGeechan. His successful track record goes back beyond the 1990 Grand Slam to the successful 1989 Lions tour to Australia and he's widely regarded as the most astute rugby brain in Britain. His side may no longer be regarded as amongst the best four in the world (as it may have been in 1990), but with careful planning and strategy, McGeechan could be the man to guide Scotland right through to the final.

Wales

The Welsh are anticipating the World Cup with delight . . . and concern! How else could it be when Britain's most passionate and knowledgeable fans have the prospect of an international rugby festival on their doorstep, yet the very real possibility that their own team's part in it will be incidental?

The regret in the valleys must be that the World Cup came some 20 years too late. Wales won or shared in ten Five Nations championships between 1964 and 1979 . . . since then, there's been just one half share – in 1988 – with the last two seasons bringing only the humiliation of the wooden spoon. Placed third in the 1987 World Cup, Wales know that their best realistic hope for 1991 appears only to be a quarter final place – and even that comes without guarantees!

After a successful pre-1990/91 season tour of Namibia, there was only depression by the time March came around. The 36–3 Five Nations defeat by France at the Parc des Princes was their heaviest ever and took their total number of points conceded for the Championship to over a hundred for the first time. Captain Paul Thorburn described the Paris match as the hardest he'd ever played in. "Whether there are better players in Wales is very debatable," he added; "I can't say I'm looking forward to facing Australia in the summer!"

The tour to Australia just a few months before the World Cup will have given the latest, highly relevant, form guide (Australia also play in Pool 3) but the chances are that Welsh optimism will not be resurfacing. What's gone wrong?

At every level, it seems, there have been substantial problems. In schools, the general decline in the teaching and coaching of team games through the 80's hit rugby – and Wales – in particular.

Glen George repels the English at Cardiff – January '91

The Welsh Squad against Ireland at Cardiff Arms Park – February '91

The conveyor belt of young talent simply stopped rolling.

The talent that had emerged then, frequently found the temptations of Rugby League too great to ignore. Hadley, Davies, Griffiths, Devereux, Young . . . just some of the names that have been lost to the professional game since 1987.

And perhaps just as damaging . . . the fall-out, still being felt, of the Welsh Rugby Union's self-inflicted scandal over the 1989 South African Centenary celebrations. Ten players went to South Africa . . . many had said they wouldn't, and a crisis in the WRU was the result, with both the secretary and president resigning.

Roy Waldron, of Wales' top club Neath, was appointed coach midway through the 89/90 season in succession to John Ryan, but his efforts to build a more mobile pack on the "Neath principle" came unstuck, particularly in that match in Paris.

Afterwards he said he had no intention of resigning – "they'll have to kick me out" – and he stood by his players, saying they'd played to their ability. "But we have limitations within our team."

The fact is that Wales have had few players of true international class in recent years . . . Paul Thorburn is one, a full-back of great determination and conviction who's one of only six internationals to pass the 300 point mark. He took over the captaincy from Robert Jones, who was controversially dropped. In the pack, Phil Davies stands out; a dominant figure, he's been played almost everywhere in the back five!

Wales' first match is, in theory, their easiest . . . against Western Samo, but the night fixture against Argentina will prove much more tricky if the Pumas have managed to add anything to their largely unhappy tour of 1990. Two victories would see Wales through to the knock-out stage, whatever happens against Australia, but Wales' second World Cup looks sadly almost certain to fall some way short of the achievements of their first.

Lock Glyn Llewellyn gets there first against Scotland at Murrayfield – February '91

Ieuan Evans

July 23rd 1989 was the day that Ieuan Evans thought his career was over. He lay on the treatment table in the British Lions' dressing room at Ballymore as his team-mates played out the remainder of their match against the ANZAC XV. Evans had dislocated his right shoulder for the fourth time in four years after tackling Michael Lynagh. The shoulder was re-set there and then but the view was that premature retirement was inevitable just at a time when Evans was proving his international class.

Fortunately, in the long term, the predictions were wrong. Although his 1990 season was an unhappy one with further injury setbacks and complete absence from the Wales side, he came back for all four matches in this year's Five Nations championship. Wales' poor season left him tryless but Evans' track record suggests that – if he gets enough of the ball – he could still be a force for Wales in the World Cup.

Evans was always a consistent try-scorer for Llanelli in the late 80's with 27 in season 86/87 and then 23 the following season. In between there was the World Cup campaign in New Zealand, where the highlight of his five matches was a record-equalling four tries against Canada. It was at that time that Rugby League clubs appeared to be taking a keen interest in him, but it came to nothing. As his international career flourished, he was selected for the Lions' tour to Australia. He played in all three Test Matches, scoring the vital try in the decisive third match.

More recently Evans was involved in controversy over the game's amateurism laws when he appeared along with two colleagues in the England match programme advertising rugby kit. No-one was paid for the advert, but it raised – once again – the thorny issue of amateurism and England's players went on 'interview-strike' later that afternoon. Evans himself urged clarification on the issue but the Welsh Rugby Union's view is largely tolerant in these matters. It has more pressing concerns *on* the pitch, where Evans' pace and skill is urgently needed.

Ieuan EVANS (WALES)

Born: March 21st 1964
Height: 5ft 10in
Weight: 13st
Occupation: Sales representative
Position: Wing
Club: Llanelli
International debut: 1987 v France
Caps: 22
International points: 28
Other honours: 3 British Lions Caps. Holds joint Welsh record for most tries in one international (4 v Canada in 1987)

Serge Blanco

If there's a sentimental choice for Player of the 1991 World Cup, then it must be Serge Blanco. For a long time his stated intention has been retirement after France's last game of the tournament, and although it's hard to imagine international rugby without him, his adoring French fans (including President Mitterand) will have to face it.

Blanco left Twickenham in March after the Grand Slam showdown saying that he had just one more match to play there. Given the draw for the World Cup, he could only mean the Final! Certainly the first French try against England, started by Blanco inside his own deadball line, was worthy of any grand occasion. It was just one of countless moments of skill and imagination that have come to Blanco. An athlete, yes; fast, agile, strong . . . but also one of rugby's greatest ball players.

In the match before, against Wales, Blanco had shown all of those qualities in the space of a magical seven seconds; receiving the ball at the end of the line, chipping ahead closely parallel to touch and then outpacing the Welsh defence over 60 yards for his 33rd international try. He'll be 33 during the World Cup but nobody's suggesting he's slowing down.

He's the nearest thing to genius in international rugby and permits himself the (sporting) eccentricity of being a heavy smoker. Otherwise, the self-obsessions of the heavily gifted have apparently passed him by. He is essentially a team man, respectful of the less eye-catching contributions of his team-mates. He is also loyal, in particular, to Jacques Fouroux, the previous French coach whose 'Rambo rugby' ideas attracted heavy criticism in the late 80's. He accepts his immense fame reluctantly, and jealously guards his family life in Biarritz.

Blanco has already been a star performer in the World Cup with his late try in the 1987 semi-final against Australia being the best in rugby's 'greatest ever game'. Blanco is back for an 'encore', before the final 'adieu'.

Serge BLANCO (FRANCE)

Born: 31st August 1958
Height: 6ft
Weight: 13st 2lbs
Occupation: Marketing executive
Position: Full-back
Club: Biarritz
International debut: 1980 v South Africa
Caps: 85 (an international record)
International points: 213 (33 tries, 6 conversions, 21 penalty goals, 2 drop goals)
Other honours: Blanco's 33 tries are the most ever scored in internationals by a Frenchman

France

Didier Camberabero

Exhilarating, daring, inventive, enigmatic . . . but ultimately unsuccessful. That was the story of France's 1991 Five Nations season, but will it be the story of their 1991 World Cup campaign?

Contrasts and contradictions abound in French rugby, but the greatest was on the pitch itself with a back division of immense class and experience, but a pack of neither, whose limitations were exposed against England in the Grand Slam decider. That 19–21 defeat at Twickenham starkly illustrated rugby's greatest truism: that no matter the brilliance of the backs, it's the possessional and territorial attrition of forward play that wins matches.

France scored three tries to England's one at Twickenham; one of them (St. André's) was out of this world, another (Mesnel's) was exceptional, yet the forwards were always outplayed, often indisciplined and rarely productive. Five of the Twickenham pack had 18 caps between them . . . of the others only Roumat, the Dax lock and Ondarts, the prop from Biarritz, look certain to feature in the World Cup. The flanker Blond, however, played throughout the Five Nations tournament to finish with five caps; he, too, looks a must for the World Cup.

But France's disarray up front was, to some extent, a transitional legacy of the Jacques Fourroux era of the 80's, a period since discredited for its ultimate over-reliance on forward strength and power. After a disappointing 1990 championship, "Rambo rugby" was finally buried late in the year after a heavy and humiliating 3–24 defeat in the 1st Test against New Zealand in Nantes. By then Daniel Dubroca was in charge, assisted by the former centre Jean Trillo to coach the backs, and although the second Test was also lost, there were enough improvements made in the early stages of the Five Nations championship to suggest that France had at last reached the turning point.

True, the victories against Ireland and Scotland had lacked real conviction, but in their third match the French simply annihilated Wales 36–3, running in six tries in a style that was nearer 7 than 15-a-side. This was the France that British rugby had long feared, but also admired. And it had been achieved without the lightning speed of Lagisquet, who had been injured against Ireland.

Pierre Berbizier clears the ball for France against Wales at Parc des Princes – March '91

The pride of France as they lined up against Wales at Parc des Princes – March '91

So the team that scored nine tries against Wales and England in the second half of the season was unchanged outside the scrum. The half-back combination of Berbizier and Camberabero played throughout the season, though his kicking doesn't have the consistency of world-class rugby. Mesnel and Sella however, are highly rated internationals, with 108 caps and 29 tries between them. St André came in at left-wing for Lagisquet and finished off the "once in a lifetime" 100 yard try against England at Twickenham and on the other wing Lafond finally established himself as first choice.

Which leaves Serge Blanco at full-back. France's captain for the World Cup has made his intentions clear. "The losers of the Pool 1 match between England and New Zealand will have lost the World Cup, because the losers will have to come to Paris to play us and we don't intend to be knocked out in the quarter finals." Blanco's post-Twickenham tally of 85 caps gave him the world record for international appearances; he's stated a clear intention to retire after the World Cup, which he's planning as a magnificent swan-song!

France, no doubt, have the easiest ride of all the top nations to the quarter finals. If they don't qualify as Pool 4 winners, then there will be a national outcry! Beyond that, the path is potentially steep, despite Blanco's assertion. England have beaten France on their three previous meetings, New Zealand won the 1990 Test Series in France. And if they do win that quarter final, then there's a semi at Murrayfield, probably against Scotland and certainly not a walk-over.

If a neutral observer exists for the World Cup (a doubtful proposition) then a French victory might well give him most pleasure. One thing is for certain; if France do win the World Cup, it will be because flair, imagination and courage have finally had their day!

Ireland

Ireland, joint wooden spoonists in the 1991 Five Nations Championship, would seem set for further disappointment in the World Cup and yet many see them as "dark horses"! Priced at 40/1 some six months before the tournament, it's a bet that might just give a run for its money!

Ireland's Five Nations results – three losses and one spectacular 21–all draw against Wales – fail to do justice to their performances. The Scottish coach Ian McGeechan said after his side's 28–25 win, "They were more positive than us, but we ended up with the points." Against England, Ireland were ahead until seven minutes from time before England eventually took the match 16–7, and there was honourable defeat against France in a see-saw match which again went to the final minutes before a 21–13 defeat. They played all their fixtures with imagination and ambition, scoring

Rob Saunders clears for Ireland against England at Lansdowne Road – March '91

ten championship tries, twice as many as the Grand Slam winners!

There may well have been a problem of staying-power (a not inconsiderable difficulty in a month-long tournament!), but under the guidance of Ciaran Fitzgerald, this is a team which may well develop further to surprise many during the World Cup. Fitzgerald pronounced himself "obviously disappointed, but also encouraged and heartened" at the end of the season as he looked forward to a tour of Namibia and then the World Cup.

In a Five Nations season in which Ireland introduced nine new caps, no

Alain Rolland prepares to pass against Argentina at Lansdowne Road – October '90

The Irish Squad against Argentina at Cardiff – October '90

debut was more eye-catching than that of the London-Irish scrum-half Rob Saunders, who also won the captaincy in Ireland's opening match against France. Saunders is a natural athlete, his pass is quick and he survived the responsibilities of his first international season well.

But the stars of the Ireland side were outside him; Brendan Mullin at centre and Simon Geoghegan on the right wing. Mullin's try in Edinburgh was the 15th of his career, breaking a 60 year-old Irish record, and in Geoghegan, Ireland have unearthed another world-class talent. He, too, made his debut against France; he didn't score . . . but one try per match came his way in the other three games. He has a jinking run which has drawn comparison with Trevor Ringland and David Duckham. His reaction was typical "I'm flattered, but I'm always critical of my own performance and I'm still learning."

Fitzgerald was at pains to point out that all of the season's new caps had performed well. This, certainly, had cleared his thoughts for the task ahead; compared to Wales, Ireland's rebuilding process had established considerable momentum.

However, one crucial position will have to be re-filled before the World Cup. In the week after the Five Nations Championship, stand-off Brian Smith went to Rugby League. Smith – an Australian by birth, had only qualified for Ireland because of his ancestry, and he returned to Sydney on a two-year contract with Balmain. His kicking had been inconsistent and Ireland's need to find a reliable penalty-taker became even more urgent.

If it was Irish backs that stole the headlines in a season of glorious failure, the forwards also made some impact, especially in the match against England. The championship's most effective pack were stifled for over three quarters of the game by the Irish eight, where Phil Matthews especially stood out in the back row. The second row combination of Rigney and Francis that finished the season was also a potent force.

Ireland will return to Murrayfield for their last match in Pool 2, with the winners likely to face a quarter final match against Wales at Murrayfield (quite an incentive for the Scots!) and the losers surely set for a fixture against Australia at Lansdowne Road. Their preference would surely be for Wales at Murrayfield, yet any fixture in front of their passionate crowd – against even the second favourites – is winnable. Ireland won't win the World Cup, but they may well cause a surprise or two!

Simon Geoghegan

The World Cup became a richer event on March 25th of this year as that was the day Simon Geoghegan turned down a lucrative offer from the English Rugby League club, Warrington, to join them as a professional. In the meantime other bids will have surely come his way but the hope is that the Irish find of 1991 will remain loyal to the Union code.

He will have just turned 23 by the time the World Cup gets under way. He is a shy, unassuming young man, was educated at St. Edmund's College in Ware, Hertfordshire and then went on to Law School in London. It was hardly a typical Irish pedigree, but his father's roots are in County Galway and so after representing his county XV at schoolboy level and then Wasps, he decided to join London Irish. Success came at various levels of international rugby, including the under-25s and the "B" team, where he scored debut tries.

However, the big breakthrough into the full international side came in January of this year when an injury to Keith Crossan allowed Geoghegan into the pre-season training squad, from which he was picked for his full debut against France at Lansdowne Road in January. This was a unique international for him as he didn't score! By the end of the Five Nations championship he'd scored three tries – one in each of the remaining three matches – and he's already established a world-wide reputation as a winger of pace and skill.

He summed up his debut season as simply 'unbelievable', adding that he owed his scoring opportunities to the attacking kind of game that the Irish were playing. Naturally, he was optimistic about Ireland's chances in the World Cup and there's no doubt that Geoghegan will feature strongly if Ireland's expansive style continues. A Geoghegan burst down the wing could be one of the World Cup's most memorable moments!

Simon GEOGHEGAN (IRELAND)

Born: 1st September 1968
Height: 6ft 1in
Weight: 13st
Occupation: Law student
Position: Right-wing
Club: London Irish
International debut: 1991 v France
Caps: 4
International points: 12 (3 tries)

Rugby Quiz

1. Who does this describe? Born in Israel, educated at Blackrock College and Trinity College, Dublin and Oxford University. Currently a stockbroker.

2. Which All Black missed the 1987 World Cup semi-final against France because of his religion?

3. Which international rugby player was only prevented from competing in the 1980 Olympics by the anti-Moscow boycott?

4. Which English club welcomed a former New Zealand captain in the 1990/91 season?

5. Which international player is a policeman in Blackpool?

6. The England coach Roger Uttley is Head of Games at which famous English public school?

7. Who benefitted from the first match ever to be played at Twickenham on a Sunday?

8. Which teams played in the French Revolution Bicentennial Match in October 1989 and what was the result?

9. Which team that appeared in the 1987 World Cup isn't in the 1991 tournament?

10. Which famous international described being dropped as "a kick in the guts"?

11. Which former England cricket captain was associated with the English Rugby Union team in season 1990/91 and why?

12. In which city is the Velez Sarsfield Stadium?

13. What was unique about Gary Chalmers' performance for Scotland in their 32–12 win over Wales in the Five Nations Championship this year?

14. Which long-serving (but little capped) Australian hooker retired before the 1991 season because of injury?

15. Who appeared to be on the verge of leaving England in the week after the Grand Slam?

16. Which European international was born in Caracas, Venezuela?

17. Who plays for France, but can't play for them in the World Cup?

18. Which record did Brendan Mullin break in Ireland's 1991 championship match with Scotland at Murrayfield?

19. Which Five Nations country has won the most Grand Slams and how many?

20. Which two members of the England team went to Barnard Castle school?

ANSWERS

1. Brendan Mullin of Leinster and Ireland.
2. Michael Jones. He's a committed Christian who believes that Sunday (the day the semi-final was played) should be a day of rest.
3. Steve McDowell, the New Zealand player, who was due to compete in the judo event.
4. Northampton, where Wayne Shelford arrived in the autumn of 1990.
5. Wade Dooley, England's second row forward.
6. Harrow.
7. The Romanian Rugby Union. Over half a million pounds was raised in gate receipts from the match between the four Home Unions and The Rest of Europe in April 1990.
8. France 27 British Lions 29.
9. Tonga.
10. Wayne Shelford, who made the remark when he was not selected for New Zealand's 1990 tour of France.
11. Bob Willis, who was hired (and then fired) as the players' agent.
12. Buenos Aires.
13. He scored one try, one drop goal, one penalty and one conversion.
14. Mark McBain, who won seven test caps in eight years.
15. Geoff Cooke, the team manager, who confirmed that he'd applied for two jobs in English county cricket, but then two days later withdrew his applications.
16. Serge Blanco of Biarritz and France.
17. Abdelatif Benazzi, who played for Morocco, his country of birth, in the World Cup qualifying rounds.
18. George Stephenson's 60 year-old Irish record of 14 international tries.
19. Wales, eight times.
20. Rory Underwood and Rob Andrew.

World Cup 53

Argentina..........

The Romanian Squad at Murrayfield – December '89

Almost two years after the bloodiest of the 1989 revolutions in Eastern Europe, there will be a special welcome at the World Cup for **Romania**. The sport lost five men during the fighting, amongst them the former Romanian captain Florica Murariu, who led his side to their historic win over Wales in 1988. Romania are in Pool 4, with a tough first match against France in Beziers; yet they will draw on the memory of a moving 12–6 victory over the French in Auch in early 1990, not only their first win on French soil, but France's first home defeat by an emerging rugby nation. Romania reached Pool 4 after achieving second place in the European Zone Qualifying tournament, beating Holland and Spain, but losing to Italy. Their style was largely orthodox, erring sometimes on the side of over-caution, but amongst those standing out (literally) were the 6ft 7½in lock forward Costica Cojecariu, who matches his immense advantage at the line-out with strength and speed in the loose. In Gheorghe Ion, the team had a hooker of potential world class and Stefan Chirila was their one back of real international ability. Pool 4 is the most open of them all; the quarter finals may not be beyond them.

Italy find themselves in Pool 1 along with England and New Zealand, a tough reward for winning the European Zone with a clean sweep against Holland, Spain and Romania! Their success was largely built on the kicking accuracy of

Zimbabwe

full-back Luigi Troiani, a player of genuine international standing, who is also a confident runner in the line. Another prominent member of the side is the loose-head prop Massimo Cuttita. His twin brother Marcello is also an international (he featured in the Italian side that competed in the 1987 World Cup), although he missed the Zone matches through injury. Rugby seems to run in the family, scrum-half Ivan Francescato is the youngest of four brothers to have played for his country and is rated as a bright prospect. And if the inexperienced Gianbattista Croci survives to the World Cup, he will be one of the tallest men in the tournament. This lock-forward is 6ft

Italy's Squad versus England at Rovigo – May '90

8in tall, but athletic and agile with it!

Italy's young side is coached by the Frenchman Bertrand Foucarde, who made his name at Tarbes, one of France's top clubs. They will come to the World Cup following a warm-up programme that includes a tour of Namibia; that in itself will do nothing to alter the view that only one win – against the USA – is the best they can hope for.

Italy's captain, Covi in action against England at Rovigo – May '90

Western Samoa – absent in 1987 – are the only newcomers to the World Cup Finals. They won their way into Pool 3 with a clean sweep of the Asian Pacific Zone qualifying tournament by beating Tonga, Korea and Japan. In their three games they scored an impressive 121 points whilst conceding only 21, and were led by prop forward Peter Fatiolofa, who has been on two previous tours to Britain. His experience has also been widened by playing club rugby in New Zealand with Ponsonby. Several other members of the squad also play in New Zealand and Australia.

Western Samoa's strength is expected to be in its backs; stand-off Philip David Saena, centres John Ah Kuoi and Too Manoo all caught the eye in the qualifying matches and Timo Tagaloa is a hugely powerful runner on the right wing. If they can be provided with a good platform by the pack, which has yet to reach its full potential, then they

World Cup 55

The Western Samoa Squad at Lansdowne Road – October '88

might stretch Australia and Wales. Their meeting with Wales at the Arms Park on 6th October will be the first in the World Cup for both sides, and an upset would throw the pool wide open.

Japan lost 11–37 to Western Samoa in the qualifying competition but second place was good enough to put them in Pool 2. The team has progressed well in the run-up to the World Cup, about which the coach Hiroaki Shukuzawa appears to be taking a realistic view. His aim is victory against Zimbabwe in the last match of the qualifying phase in Belfast; that, he believes, would be enough in itself to increase his team's international standing. Over the last three years he's worked closely with the team captain Seiji Hirao, who finished the qualifying tournament with 24 caps, playing at both stand-off and centre. Hirao also played a season with Richmond in south-west London in 1985.

Japan's scrum is likely to be its strong point, especially in the front five. Vice-captain Tsuyoshi Fujita – the experienced hooker – is influential at

Zimbabwe put Scotland's Iain Paxton under pressure at Wellington – May '87

Japan's Toshitaki Kimura beats Australia's Simon Poidevin to the ball in Sydney – June '87

line-outs; he does the throwing and second-row forward Atsushi Oyagi does the catching, and will be looking to impose himself on the tournament as a world-class player. And in Takahiro Hosokawa, Japan have a fine all-rounder at full-back, as much a runner as a kicker. Japan's first match is against Scotland on the first Saturday of the World Cup; Japan will be looking to draw on the inspiration of recent memories – in 1989 Japan beat Scotland by 28 points to 24!

Rugby is in its 102nd year in **Zimbabwe,** where the game is predominantly played at schoolboy level by young blacks, a reversal of the colonial days of Rhodesia. Those changes are now increasingly reflected in the national side which convincingly won the African Zone qualifying round with straight victories over Ivory Coast, Morocco and Tunisia, scoring 62 points and conceding 22. It was led by scrum-half Andy Ferreira, who emerged as the player of the tournament and his country's most capped player with 22 appearances. He's also a very useful tennis coach!

The wingers Bedford Chimbima and Zivanai Dzinomurumbi also featured. Both are electrifyingly quick with Chimbima an especially popular and powerful try-scorer. Three names stood out in the pack; Peter Albasini, the hooker, is an effective combatant in the loose, lock Anthony Horton is fast and mobile, a potential world-class player, and flanker, Brendan Dowson is also well regarded. Zimbabwe lived up to their ranking as number two – 500/1 outsiders. In the 1987 World Cup in Pool 2 against Scotland and Ireland, they will be similarly rated.

Canada, though, must feel they have a chance of reaching the quarter finals from Pool 4, which – in France – contains only one "first-class" international side, along with Fiji and Romania. Qualification for this pool was Canada's reward for topping the Americas' Zone preliminary round, which they sealed with a stirring 19–15 victory in Buenos Aires over Argentina. The coach Ian Birtwell described it as "the most important match in the history of the game in this country" and left Canada with three wins (two against the Pumas and one against the USA) and a

The Argentina Squad against Ireland at Lansdowne Road, October '90

surprising defeat by the USA in Seattle, (more to come shortly).

Canada were led in two matches by full-back Mark Wyatt, who finished the preliminary round as the country's most capped current player with 20 internationals to his credit. He likes to use a rubber ring as a tee for his place kicks, so look out for controversy in the World Cup. The Canadian squad is largely composed of British Columbians and two of them will contest the stand-off position with special rival Gareth Rees, a fine kicker of the ball and his fellow University of Victoria student Bobby Ross, more able as a passer. Canada's advantage is that they play France last in Pool 4.

If second is nowhere in American sport then the **United States** are surely bound for double-oblivion! They've been drawn in the toughest Pool – 1 – against New Zealand and England after coming last in the Americas Zone preliminary round. Yet they did score that morale-boosting 14–12 victory in Seattle against Canada, a result which was against the run of play but which nevertheless gave them some self-respect. This wasn't exactly a settled side, altogether 32 players were used in the four matches, with only prop Chris Lippert, lock Kevin Swords and the former England Under-23 international, centre Mark Williams, playing in all four games.

Yet the enormity of the task facing the USA team became fully clear on last year's tour to Australia; although the Eagles won three state matches, they were thrashed by the Wallabies 67–9, their biggest margin of defeat in eight years. That was followed, though, by a successful three-match tour of Japan, which included a 25–15 Test match win in which scrum-half Barry Daily took over the captaincy from number eight Brian Vizard. Both have been prominent members of a squad which makes up in athleticism for what it lacks in experience. The USA's first Pool 1 game is in Otley against Italy . . . if it proves to be a parallel to the soccer team's 1990 World Cup fixture in Rome (a narrow 1–0 defeat), then even that may prove to be a considerable achievement!

Argentina are in Pool 3 and return to the British Isles just a year after a disappointing tour which ended in a clean sweep of international defeats and controversy. The margin against Ireland was narrow enough – 18–20 – but then the Pumas were overwhelmed, first by England 0–51 and then by Scotland 3–49. The match at Twickenham was also marred by the dismissal of prop-forward Frederico Mendèz, who felled Paul Ackford with a punch in full view of the television cameras. Beyond that, the tour also appeared to mark the retirement of their highly gifted veteran stand-off Hugo Porta, who limped out of the match at Murrayfield. Porta will be 40 years old when the World Cup starts. It will be amazing if he's not there and although he will want to be on the pitch, he may have to settle for the sidelines!

Kevin Higgins of the USA against Ireland in New York – September '89

Yet, the previous August, Argentina had beaten England 15–13 in Buenos Aires with a different team nucleus, though England were also much-changed. The only conclusion is that Argentinian strategy – both on and off the field – is in a state of flux. Lack of height in the line-out is likely to be just one of several problems for Argentina, who will be thrown into the deep-end at Stradey Park in the second match of the tournament against Australia. One victory (against Western Samoa) appears to be their best hope, though they may fancy their chances against Wales.

Fiji remain the mystery – an unpredictable mixture of adventurism, excitement, indiscipline and violence. Their last match in England (in 1989) ended in defeat by 58 points to 23 and the dismissal of two players. Yet they scored four tries in the match with the occasional burst of exhilarating running rugby. A week earlier they'd been beaten by Scotland 38–17. More recently, though, came victory in the Hong Kong Sevens tournament, a form of the game best suited to their open style. Names to watch out for are Serevi, Nadruku, Koroduadua and their 6ft 4in forward Rasari, who has the speed of a winger!

Their automatic entry to the 1991 World Cup was an entitlement from their quarter-final appearance in '87, but Western Samoa, who beat them 30–17 in June 1990, will begrudge them the Pacific's one seeded place. Nevertheless, Fiji were taken on for a while in their World Cup build-up by the former Australian coach Alan Jones and they enter Pool 4 with as good a chance as Canada or Romania of reaching the quarter finals as runners-up to France.

Fiji fight for the ball with New Zealand at Christchurch – May '87

Rugby Trivia.....

The Wales v Argentina match on Wednesday 9th October 1991 (kick-off 8.00 pm) will be the first Rugby Union international played at Cardiff Arms Park under floodlights.

England's players mischievously celebrated their Grand Slam victory at Twickenham with an impromptu dressing-room chorus of the song *We're in the Money*. A nice touch, given the season's rows over "communication for reward"!

The African Zone qualifying match between Morocco and the Ivory Coast was abandoned after 70 minutes because of a mass brawl between the two teams. Morocco were leading 11–4 at the time.

Simon Hodgkinson's seven penalties against Wales in England's 25–6 win in January set a new world record for successful penalties in any one international match.

The back division of Racing Club de France all wore pink bow-ties and brightly coloured shorts during their 1990 club championship final with Agen! They also drank champagne at half-time . . . and won the match by 22 points to 12!

160 random drug tests will be undertaken on players before the World Cup. A further two players will be tested from each side at every match during the competition. Any player who tests positive will be banned from future participation and would then be subject to further disciplinary action from his home union.

The international record distance for place kicking belongs to Wales' Paul Thorburn. He landed a massive 64.22 metre penalty against Scotland in 1986 at Cardiff Arms Park.

Adidas have won the contract to supply all World Cup matches with the official ball. Research and development of the ball took three years and Adidas claim that its new aerodynamic shape will mean greater passing and kicking accuracy.

Britain's most famous TV rugby commentator, Bill McLaren, will be working on radio for the Rugby World Cup. ITV, the host broadcasters, failed to persuade him to leave the BBC and work for them; instead, he can be heard on BBC Radio 5, the Sports Network.

All referees for the World Cup will have been judged beforehand by a special referees' assessment panel. There had been criticism of the appointment and performance of some referees in the '87 event.

The last time England played Fiji (at Twickenham in 1989) it resulted in the first double sending-off in 118 years of international rugby. Fiji's Tevita Vonolagi and Noa Nadruku were both dismissed for violent play.

Each live World Cup match will be covered by 12 ITV cameras, including 4 mobile cameras. Half-time intervals will last at least five minutes to accomodate advertising breaks.

The first French try against England at Twickenham this year (often referred to as the best try ever seen at the ground) took 17¼ seconds from the moment the ball crossed the French line to St. André's touchdown.

Diversionary tactics – the French cockerel on the pitch at Cardiff

Britain's sports loving Prime Minister John Major sent a special message from Bermuda, where he was meeting with President Bush, to congratulate the England team on their Grand Slam. It read "Congratulations on a performance of great authority. Let's hope you can carry on to success in the World Cup."

Laurent Seigne, Louis Armary and Pascal Ondarts – the French front-row in the infamous first Test against New Zealand last year – took the field with cuts and bruises to their faces. They'd been self-inflicted! The three men had been head-butting each other in the changing room in an effort to psyche themselves up!

Although the International Board decided that the rules of the game should not be amended before the World Cup, afterwards it will consider awarding five points for a try. The idea is to increase the differential between the value of the try and the penalty kick.

As many as 4,500 media representatives are expected to be accredited for the World Cup. The accreditation dead-line was six months before the start of the tournament!

The new North Stand at Twickenham, the venue for the World Cup Final, is the second highest building of its type in Europe.

Some countries will be receiving television coverage of the World Cup free of charge, because they simply can't afford it. Czechoslovakia, Yugoslavia and the Soviet Union are amongst them.

The World Cup Message Relay was conceived as a publicity-stunt to announce the tournament. It's similar to the Olympic torch concept. A rugby ball, containing the "World Cup Message", will have passed by hand through all give host countries by October 3rd. Rugby School, the birthplace of the game, was chosen as the starting point . . . the relay ends at Twickenham.

.....did you know?

Rugby's New Age

The second week in October 1990 was supposed to mark the beginning of Rugby Union's "New Age" . . . a week to mark the end of the sport's long-standing confusions and inconsistencies over its taboo subject . . . money!

At last, it was thought, top players would be allowed to earn fees openly from their association with the game. The dedicated approach of the vast majority was professional in attitude, if not in fact. Why shouldn't their considerable sacrifices of time and effort be properly compensated? That was the argument already accepted by most member unions of the International Board.

Yet, when the Board met at Murrayfield and announced its new, more "liberal" (and supposedly clear-cut) regulations, what followed was simply more argument and controversy, particularly in England. Each member union was permitted to interpret the regulations as it saw fit, but the English governing body – the Rugby Football Union – stood out and strongly resisted any breach of the "ring-fence" of amateurism around the game.

So in the build-up to the World Cup, an event from which anything up to £25 million will pour into the game, the English players' ability to earn was still severely curtailed. Rugby's "New Age" – big-money commercial exploitation, high-profile media coverage, large scale development of the game across the world – was happening for the administration, but not for the men who were making it all possible . . . the players.

The true spirit of rugby – with the game played above all for its unique pleasure and sense of fellowship – has

Will Carling ponders the future

always been sacrosanct. The players have never wanted to disturb that tradition; they've had no interest in being paid for playing. Yet in the eighties, as the game expanded, the Shelfords, the Guscotts and the Campeses became international stars with their names giving them real earning potential outside the game.

Inevitably, inconsistencies between the Unions quickly emerged, with the New

Zealand RFU, for instance, more tolerant in its interpretation of the existing rules than either the English or Irish bodies. Some All Blacks appeared on television endorsing products, others formed themselves into limited companies for hire as after-dinner speakers or supermarket-openers. Yet in England, rugby's "black-market economy" took hold, as some players received jobs, cars and generous expenses from clubs anxious to retain their services.

The RFU's position – that the game was essentially a spare time activity played for enjoyment and not for reward – was consistent enough (it's never wavered) The problem was that its rigorous application throughout the English game engendered bitterness and deceit, particularly from those who looked enviously at more liberal conditions in the Southern Hemisphere. The International Board, prompted both by the inconsistencies amongst the Unions and the steady drift of top players to Rugby League, eventually decided upon an attempt to clarify matters. Hence the Murrayfield meeting in October 1990.

In announcing its new Regulation 4 on October 12, the IB appeared to be taking a substantial step forward; money, it said, could be earned from any form of appearance (supermarket-openings) or communication (newspaper articles/speeches). Yet the Board then said that appearance or communication for reward must not derive from the game . . . but still left the interpretation of the regulation to the individual Union concerned!

In a sense, the game was back to square one with a new set of rules that confusingly gave with one hand and took away with the other! The Australian and New Zealand Unions appeared pleased with what had been produced. Eddie Tonks, NZRFU chairman said "It is an end to the terribly restrictive regulations; they really were out of date" . . . but in England there was soon substantial discontent from both the Rugby Football Union and the players.

The matter came to a head in a famous incident in Cardiff after the Wales v England match in January of this year. In an ill-judged gesture after their first win at the Arms Park in 28 years, the England players all refused to give TV and press interviews. They said at the time that they were too emotionally drained. It emerged afterwards that the RFU had put a general ban on any money-earning once the players were together as a squad . . . and a *particular* sanction on a £5,000 interview fee asked of the BBC. All this after apparent co-operation and conciliation between the players and the Union, who'd met on several occasions since October to thrash out a working arrangement.

The ensuing row highlighted the continuing ambiguities in the regulations which the RFU later described as unconstitutional. The International Board attempted to deal again with the matter in March 1991. It passed – unanimously – a regulation permitting after-dinner speaking for payment, re-emphasising that no player should be paid for playing . . . but still agreed that the new rule should be left to the interpretation of individual unions. It was agreed that a list of "do's and don'ts" should be drawn up in an effort to develop some kind of world-wide charter, but it was by no means certain that this would appear before the World Cup.

Rugby Union's "New Age" had failed to dawn for England's Grand Slam heroes. Only some of England's international elite found money on offer from non-rugby related activities, and amongst even them where was frustration at the RFU's attitude. Their particular complaint was that they were almost single-handedly responsible for generating the RFU's multi-million pound income (in gate receipts, TV rights fees and sponsorships).

If there was so much money swilling about in the game, why should the players not be entitled to a small share of it? And beyond that, they asked, when will there ever be a consistent and straightforward set of regulations? When indeed!